Recorder Sonatas

by J.C. Pepusch (1670-1752)

Compiled & Edited by Robert Bancalari

WWW.MELBAY.COM

Contents

Preface

Like George Frideric Handel, Johann Christoph Pepusch (1667-1752) was an 18th century German composer who lived and worked in London. He composed church music, concertos and sonatas with continuo, an accompaniment part that includes a bass line and harmony, typically played on a keyboard instrument with other instruments such as a cello or upright bass carrying the bass line. This is a collection of six of his wonderful sonatas for recorder.

Robert Bancalari

Sonata 1

Adagio

J. C. Pepusch (1667-1752)

♩ = 70

tr

5

tr

9

tr

13

16

tr

19

tr

tr

Allegro

9
13
15
19
22
25
28
32
36
39
tr

Adagio

Allegro

Sonata 2

Largo

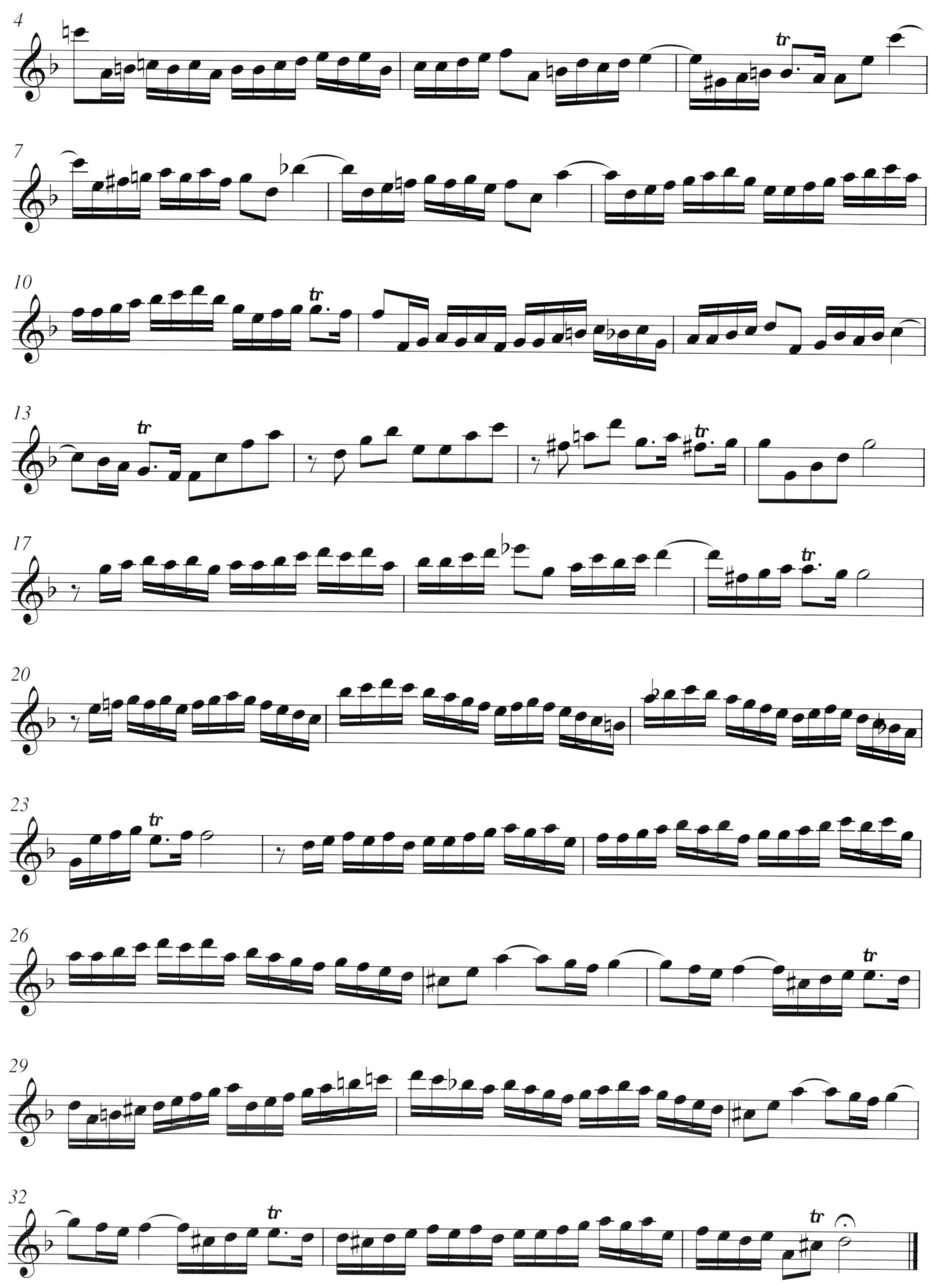
4
tr
7
10
tr
13
tr
tr
17
tr
20
23
tr
26
tr
29
32
tr
tr

Largo

Allegro

Sonata 3

Adagio

Allegro

Adagio

Allegro

♩ = 120

1

6

11

tr

16

20

tr

Sonata 4

Adagio

Allegro

Adagio

Giga

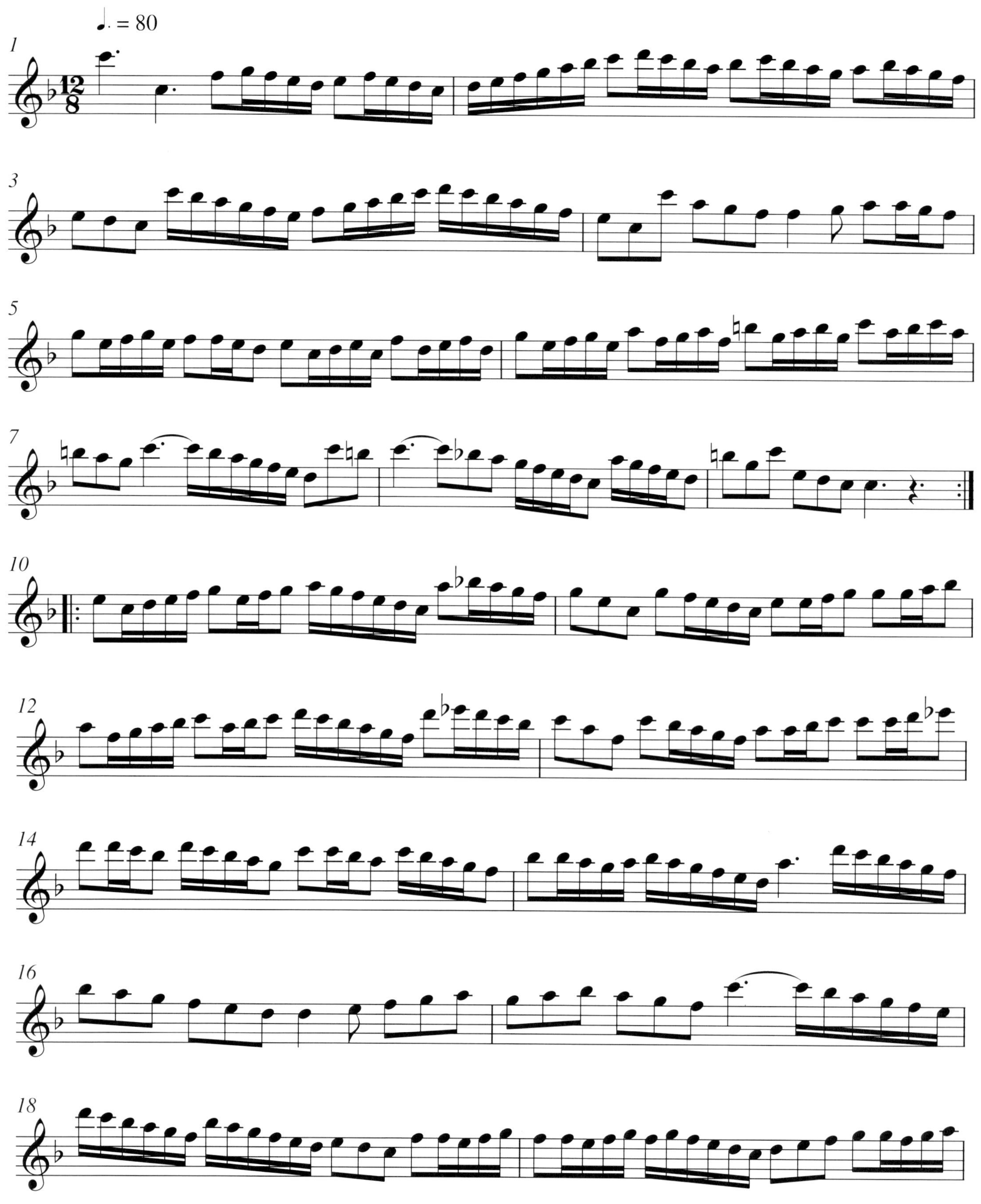

20
21

Sonata 5

Adagio

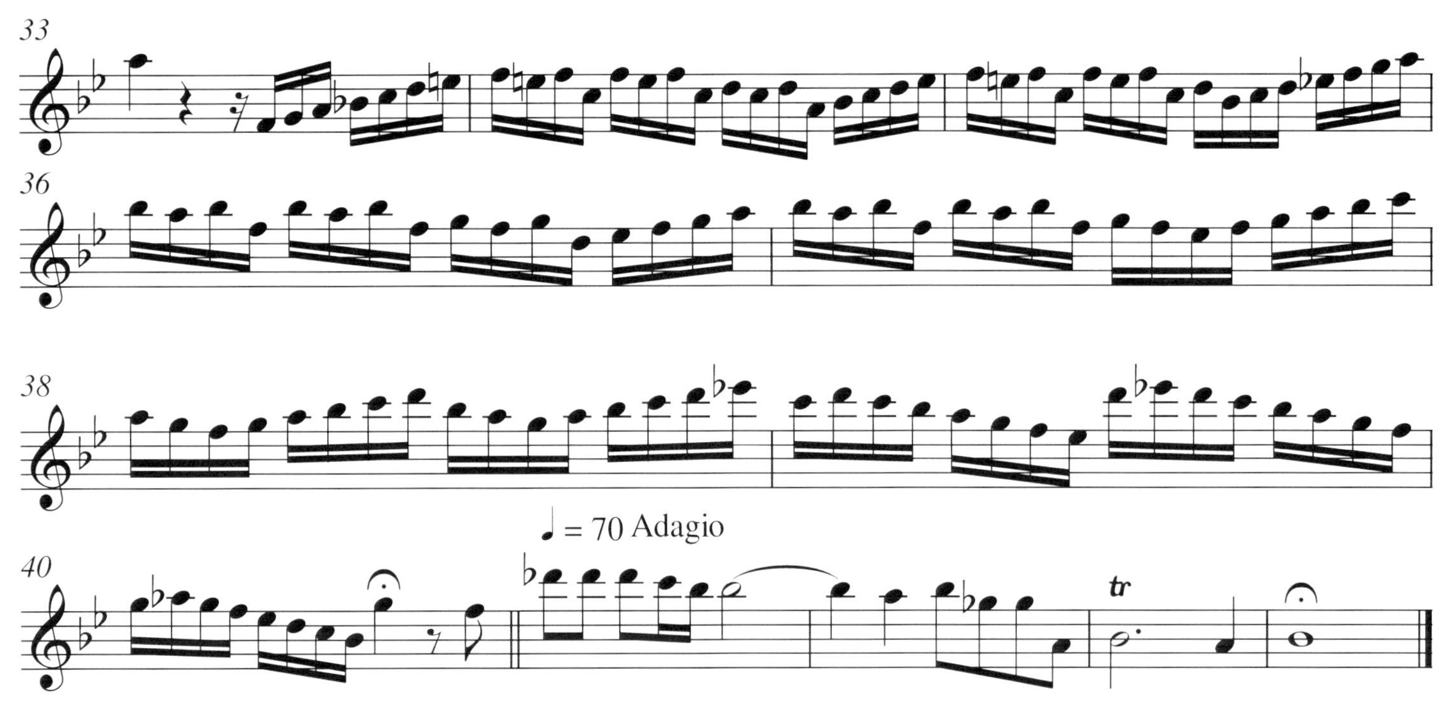
33
36
38
40
♩ = 70 Adagio
tr

Allegro

1 ♩ = 100

5 tr

8 tr

12 tr

14 tr

Adagio

Allegro

Sonata 6

Adagio

Allegro

Adagio

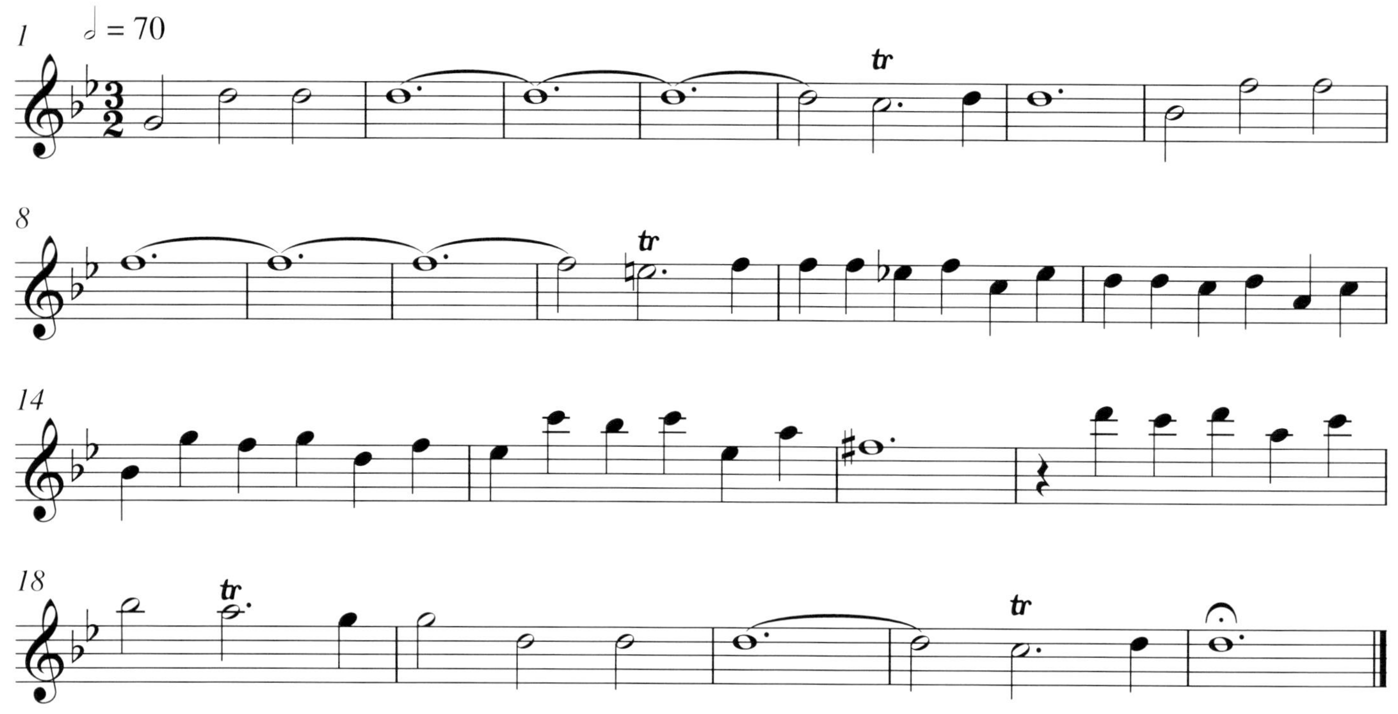

Allegro

17
Double
20
24
28
30
tr
tr

WWW.MELBAY.COM